Little Sable Point Lighthouse

Little Sable Point, at Mears, and Big Sable Point, at Ludington, are two areas of West Michigan's shoreline that meander several miles out into Lake Michigan. In the late 1800's, with increased shipping activity on Lake Michigan, the need for good lighthouses became apparent.

Building a lighthouse at Little Sable Point was no small job. Materials needed to come by boat, but without a harbor, workers first had to build docks and dredge the sand to be able to land men and supplies at the lighthouse construction site. The light station first went into service in 1874. Two of the lighthouse keepers pictured here in 1922, are Wallace Hall and Henry Olsen. The close up of Henry was taken about the time he was married in 1923. Below, two workers pose on the top railing while painting.

In the early operation of the lighthouse, many ship captains complained that the brick tower blended with the trees making it hard to see in the daytime, so the tower was painted white.

The light became automated in 1954 and without the need of a resident keeper, the dwellings were demolished the following year. The tower was returned to natural brick in 1977. A major restoration occurred twenty years later when twenty-five thousand bricks in the tower were replaced.

Standing at 115 feet above the lake level, the light from the Third Order Fresnel Lens is visible for 17 miles.

Little Sable Lighthouse at Twilight

One of the most prominent figures to leave his mark in the history of the region is Charles Mears. The village of Mears and the Charles Mears State Park bear his name.

Work opportunities in the lumber industry brought many people to the area. With no harbor, lumber sawn in Mears was shipped by railroad. The railroad, in turn, brought supplies and tourists to the area.

Pictured at the top is a circa 1900 photograph of the loggers boarding house (still standing) at the channel near Lake Michigan, and a view of the saw mill at Mears.

The area has changed a lot in the last century. During the lumbering era, most of the trees around the sand dunes were harvested, leaving behind only stumps. Then, wind and nature took over and caused the dunes to actually start moving. An early photograph shows the forest remains being covered by blowing sand. With such a simple element as sand, nature can create fantastic art forms.

The stark beauty of the patterns and textures can change from day to day. Frequent windstorms sculpt the sand into fantastic formations including caves and holes.

You may leave tracks in the sand but nature will soon erase them as if you were never there.

It is easy to understand how wind can move a sailboat but hard to imagine the same wind moving an entire sand dune. It does it one grain at a time. Prevailing westerly winds pick up sand along Lake Michigan's shore where the grains of sand will eventually migrate into Silver Lake.

Sunlight, clouds and rain make this a unique place where the scenery changes by the hour. Ripples and sand patterns always become more dramatic in the early morning and late afternoon sunlight. Without trees, the vast expanse seems endless.

The above aerial photograph shows the sweeping curve of Little Sable Point shoreline and the long fingers of dunes in the process of filling in Silver Lake and covering the forest. On the north edge of the dunes, the sand has moved more than 1,200 feet since 1940. During that time, a number of homes have been moved away and approximately ten houses have been covered. There are also seventeen automobiles buried under the sand! The story is that Bill's Dune Rides would place a car partway down a dune so passengers could run down the dune to stop and look at the car. With a dated note in the glovebox, each year another car would be placed on the dune because the previous car would have been completely covered by sand.

In spite of the desert-like conditions and unstable sand, life does exist on the dunes. Some grasses have deep roots with as much as 90% of the plant being underground.

Here and there wildflowers will bloom brightly. White-tailed deer and other animals regularly frequent the dunes but usually seek the cover of trees at the edges.

One of the dreams of Charles Mears was to create a harbor for shipping lumber by dredging the channel between Silver Lake and Lake Michigan. A contractor from Racine, Wisconsin was hired. Partway through the project, the dredge mysteriously burned and a harbor at Silver Lake never materialized.

The Silver Lake outlet at Lake Michigan has always been a popular beach and playground area. The shallow water is somewhat warmer than Lake Michigan and is a great place for tiny tots to play.

The scenic mile-long drive along Silver Creek leads past a few homes and cottages and ends at the lighthouse. Midway, a small dam maintains a constant water level in Silver Lake. Above the dam, a footbridge crosses to a secluded picnic area. Below the dam the shallow water is ideal for canoeing or floating downstream to Lake Michigan.

Early visitors to Silver Lake would arrive by train at Mears, then be transported to the resorts by carriage while wagons would follow with their luggage. Many would spend the entire summer at Silver Lake.

Malcolm (Mac) Wood founded Flora-dale as an American Plan resort where guests would spend an all-inclusive week with everything provided.

It was here that he started the Dune Scooter business. The dune rides became so popular he needed more space and moved the Dune Scooters closer to the dunes. Ed and Dolores Bauer purchased Flora-dale and as a team were perfect for the resort. Guests enjoyed Ed's quick wit and flare for planning entertainment and activities. Dee's cooking skills made every meal a delightful experience. The resort continued until they retired.

Pictured below is Mac Wood with a group of happy guests heading out for fun on the sand dunes.

In 1930, while at Flora-dale, Mac Wood started taking guests out on the dunes just for the fun of it. His first Dune Scooter was a Model-A Ford.

The trick was to drive in sand where one would normally get stuck! Being very innovative, Mac modified the cars to run with as many as ten wheels. Later, he went to oversized aircraft type tires with low pressure allowing them to float over the sand. Vehicle maintenance was always high, as the sand is unkind to auto parts, especially brakes and bearings.

Mac Wood had a special sense of humor that made him instantly popular. He loved to show his passengers a good time as he shared his knowledge and love of the dunes with everyone. A few stops along the way and a little dip in Lake Michigan were always a part of the trip.

The above twilight photo was taken in 1962 and was one of the first Mac Wood's post cards produced by Penrod Studio (now Penrod/Hiawatha).

Dune Scooters are custom-made four-wheel drive vehicles equipped with special tires. Each scooter can carry twenty people. The southern part of the dunes is leased by the Silver Lake State Park to Mac Wood's Dune Rides.

For thousands of visitors to Silver Lake, this is the best and easiest way to see the dunes first hand.

Scooter drivers delight in sharing the dune experience with visi-ors and pause to view ancient stumps that had been buried for nore than a century. Blowing sand has polished them and sculp-ured them into objects of art. The 40-minute ride covers about even miles of trails over great expanses of pure sand, up and own the hills and a brief encounter with Lake Michigan. There re several stops along the way to take pictures or just marvel at he natural beauty of the awesome dunes. The drivers have amed most of the dunes and the honor of being the tallest goes to azorback. They pause here just before the drop-off to Silver ake. It is a thrill to view the panorama from the top of Razorback nd even a bigger thrill plunging down the steep slope.

The dune ride is still operated by the Wood family: Mac Wood's on, Pete and his wife Bev, plus their daughters Janet, Shelby and uth Ann and her husband, Jim.

Following pages: Glowing in rich warm color of late afternoon, his view of the magnificent dunes shows the sand patterns as well s the contour of the dune formations.

Sand Dunes Panorama

Photo by: Pete Wood

Fulgurite hunting, while out on the sand dunes, may yield interesting keepsakes. If sand is heated hot enough, it melts and makes glass. When a bolt of lightning strikes a sand dune, the extreme heat from the electrical charge melts a hole in the sand leaving a tube formation with smooth glass on the inside and rough sand partly melted on the outside. The vitrified tube is called a fulgurite. The glass tube is fragile and is usually found on top of the sand after the wind has blown some of the sand away.

In 1998, after collecting fulgurites for 50 years, Pete Wood found the granddaddy of all fulgurites sticking up out of the sand after a windstorm. It is more than two inches in diameter in places and is 10 feet long; however, he and his son-in-law, Jim Foster, (pictured) could not retrieve it in one piece. The huge fulgurite is on display in the gift shop at Mac Wood's Dune Rides.

Photo by: Pete Wood

The region's annual fireworks display is set off from atop the dunes so visitors and residents can enjoy a clear view across the lake.

The influential Lathers family has long been respected in the Silver Lake region. Swift Lathers lived in Mears and gained fame as the founder and publisher of the "World's Smallest" newspaper. The Mears Newz, a 5x7 size paper, ran continuously from 1914 until his death in 1970.

Swift's son, Bill Lathers, owned a trucking business and in 1949 started Bill's Dune Rides on land previously purchased from John & Les Flood. Bill's Dune Rides became very successful and continued until 1977. The property, purchased by the State of Michigan, allowed Silver Lake State Park to double the size of the off-road vehicle portion of the park.

Bill's garage became Craig's Cruisers recreational facility and it is interesting that the phone number for Bill's Dune Rides (873-2511) has survived and continues as Craig's Cruisers' phone number.

On the scene for a while was the Silver Queen, a stern-wheel excursion boat operated by the Joe Ferwerda family. It would shuttle passengers back and forth to the dunes.

Another long time attraction was John Flood's Riding Stable.

For many years, the shipwrecked Novadoc could be seen from Juniper Beach just north of the dunes. It was driven aground in a fierce storm on November 11, 1940. Two crewmembers drowned in an attempt to reach shore. The remaining 17 men were stranded, in below freezing cold, for three days until fishermen from Pentwater risked their own lives in the wild seas to rescue the men.

Silver Lake State Park came into being in 1920 when Carrie Mears, daughter of Charles Mears, donated twenty-five acres of land, allowing the unique treasure of the Silver Lake dunes to be saved and protected for future generations. Originally people could pitch a tent and camp along the lake, now the park has 200 modern campsites.

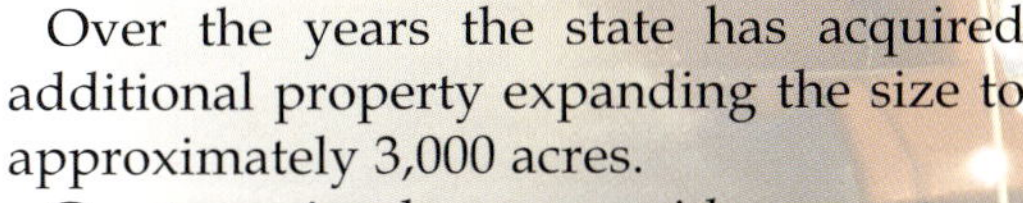

Over the years the state has acquired additional property expanding the size to approximately 3,000 acres.

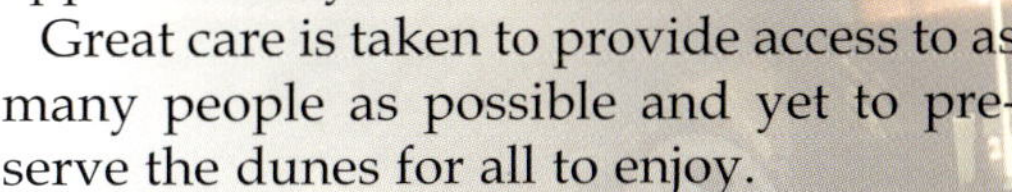

Great care is taken to provide access to as many people as possible and yet to preserve the dunes for all to enjoy.

The sand dunes area is divided into three parts. The southern section is for Mac Wood's Dune Rides, the center section is for pedestrian use and the northern portion is for off-road vehicles. Included in the park system are the beach and parking area at the Little Sable Point Lighthouse, the Charles Mears State Park at Pentwater and the Hart-Montague Bicycling and Hiking Trail.

Silver Lake Sand Dunes has become Mid-America's most popular place for off-road vehicles. Not only is the scenery spectacular, so are the challenges.

Motorcycles, quads, dune buggies, Jeeps and four-wheel drives all can share the roadless sand mountains. One should check with the state park before driving on the dunes to make sure entry and safety requirements are met. It is a wonderful family sport to cruise the dunes, then park by Lake Michigan and enjoy a swim or picnic.

One dune aptly named Test Hill, lords it over all of the others. If you can get to the top of that one, the spectacular view makes it all worth while.

There is a lot of camaraderie out on the dunes as spectators line up to watch a little friendly competition.

At the end of a day on the dunes, even with sand in ones hair and shoes, there is a magical feeling of satisfaction, a rewarding experience never to be forgotten!

The size of Silver Lake is about one mile by two and one-half miles and is ideal for swimming and other water sports.

From a misty sunrise over Silver Lake to a busy fun filled day, there are many things to do in the region.

In addition to the water and sand-related activities, the area offers plenty of food, fun and shopping. With an excellent waterfront hotel, rental cottages and great campgrounds, there are ample accommodations for everyone.

There are a number of great golf courses in the county all quite close to Silver Lake and as one might expect, with all the sand around, what else but a few sand traps!

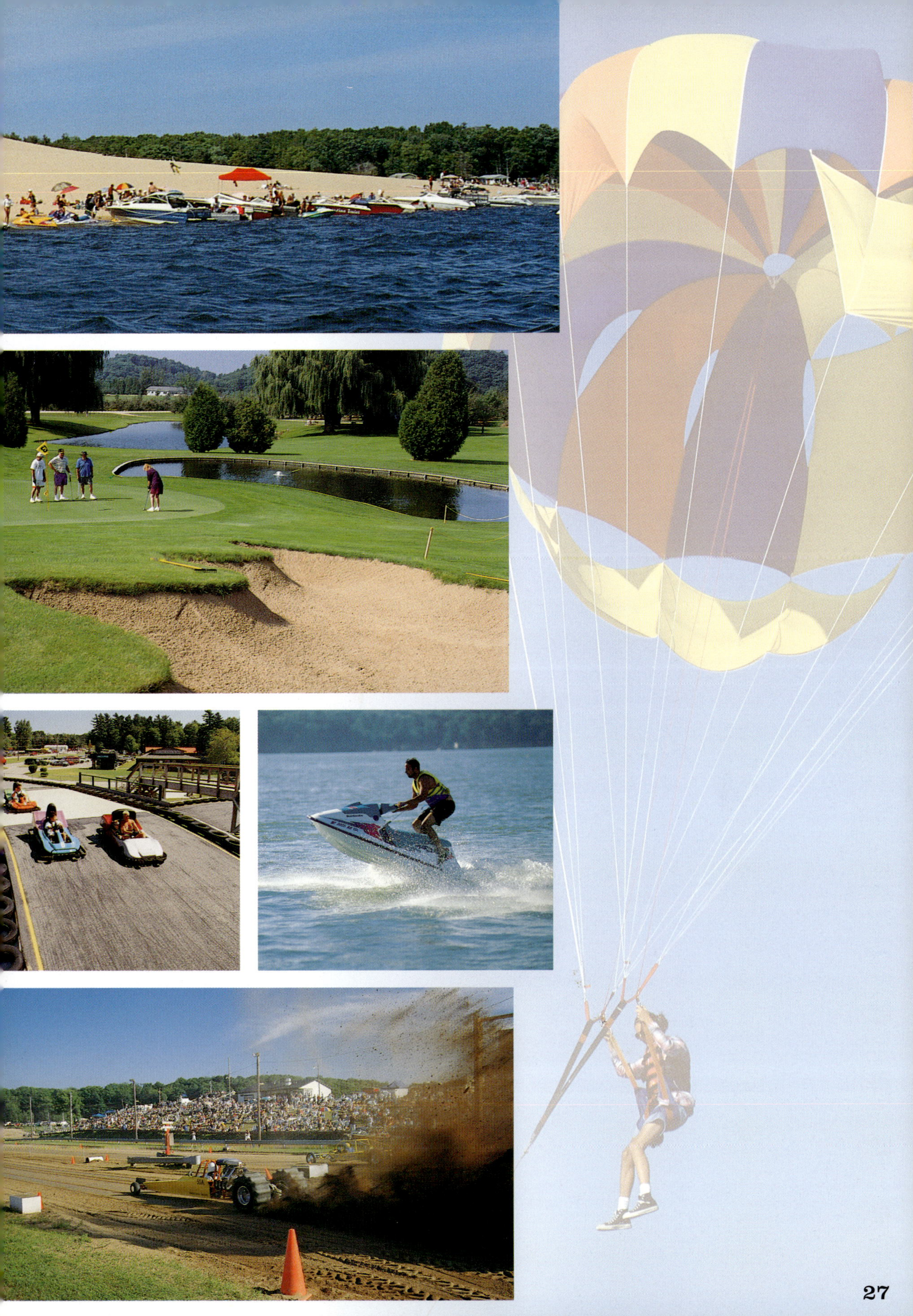

The Silver Lake region of Oceana County has ideal soil and climate conditions for growing fine fruit and vegetables.

In the springtime the white cherry blossoms are spectacular and the air is sweet with the delicate fragrance of apple blossoms.

Large quantities of sweet and tart cherries are produced here. Most tart cherries are harvested by shaking the tree and catching the cherries in a large umbrella-like device. Cherries are then transported, in large vats of cold water, to market and processing plants. This keeps them fresh and prevents the fruit from being bruised.

MICHIGAN CHERRY PIE

Pastry for 2-crust pie	1 ½ cups sugar
2 ½ cups pitted tart cherries	1 Tbsp. quick cooking tapioca
¼ cup cherry juice	
1/8 tsp. salt	1 tsp. butter

Line pie pan with pastry, put in cherries, mix juice, salt, sugar, tapioca and pour over cherries, dot with butter, put on top crust, bake at 400° F. 40 to 50 minutes.

Asparagus grows to perfection here and so much is produced that Oceana County has become the Asparagus Capital of the World. The towns of Hart and Shelby celebrate the event with an annual Asparagus Festival. It is amazing how many asparagus recipes are available.

Asparagus opens the growing season and is closely followed by strawberries and other varieties of produce. Through the summer there are many fruit and vegetable markets open. Roadside stands display everything from rhubarb, sweet cherries, and sweet corn to ever-abundant zucchini squash. Washed sweet cherries make an excellent snack and corn on the cob roasted over a campfire is hard to beat. What can taste better than a fresh tree-ripened peach?

The soil and climate conditions along Lake Michigan combine to produce fruit with better flavor than in most other parts of the country. The springtime lake effect keeps fruit tree buds from developing too soon, thus avoiding frost damage. It also tempers the autumn season.

Several farm markets feature fresh baked pies and pastries as well as locally pressed apple cider in the fall.

Driving along the U.S. 31 expressway between New Era and Hart, one can enjoy wonderful panoramic views showing hills with orchards as far as the eye can see.

There are several large food processors and a number of frozen food storage plants in the area.

Cherries ripen in July, peaches in August and apples from September on into autumn.

Photo by Woodland Farm Market

Upper Silver Lake has a meandering shoreline that provides picturesque waterfront sites for many cottages and year 'round homes.

A century ago, much of the land around Mears that had been cleared of forest was being planted with fruit trees. The country store, pictured below, was an all-important source of supplies needed for everyday life.

Today, great maple trees line the streets of Mears.

In 1869-1870, the Grand Rapids and Lakeshore Railroad came into Mears and became an important means of transportation for incoming supplies and for shipping lumber from the local saw mills.

The old photograph, taken more than a century ago, shows an 1870 wood burning steam locomotive at the Mears railroad station where trains would stop twelve times a day. With a population of 1,000 people Mears was larger than Hart or Shelby.

In 1982, the track was abandoned and has since become the Hart-Montague Bicycle Trail State Park. The 22-mile section of the old right-of-way has been paved and is used for bikers, hikers, in-line skaters, runners and snowmobilers. From Montague southward, the trail is being extended ten additional miles.

 Relaxing at Silver Lake